A LITTLE GIRL NAMED MARY ANN

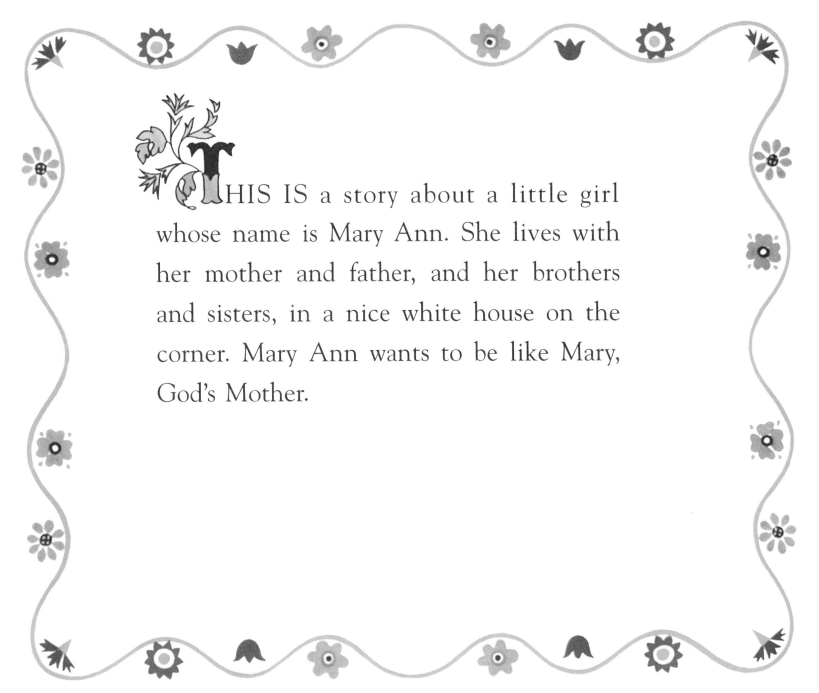

THIS IS a story about a little girl whose name is Mary Ann. She lives with her mother and father, and her brothers and sisters, in a nice white house on the corner. Mary Ann wants to be like Mary, God's Mother.

WHEN MARY ANN gets up in the morning, she says, "Today I will try to do what God wants."

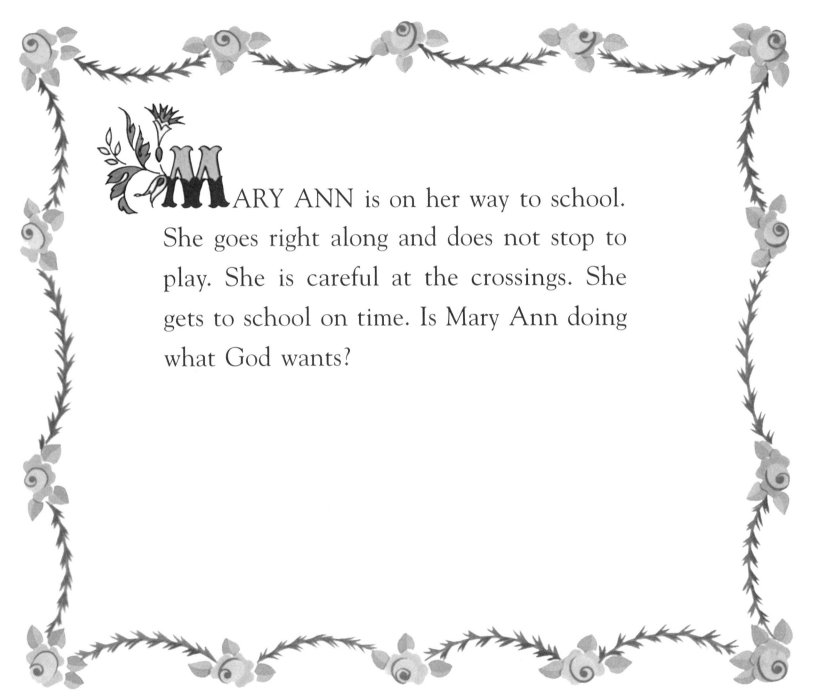

MARY ANN is on her way to school. She goes right along and does not stop to play. She is careful at the crossings. She gets to school on time. Is Mary Ann doing what God wants?

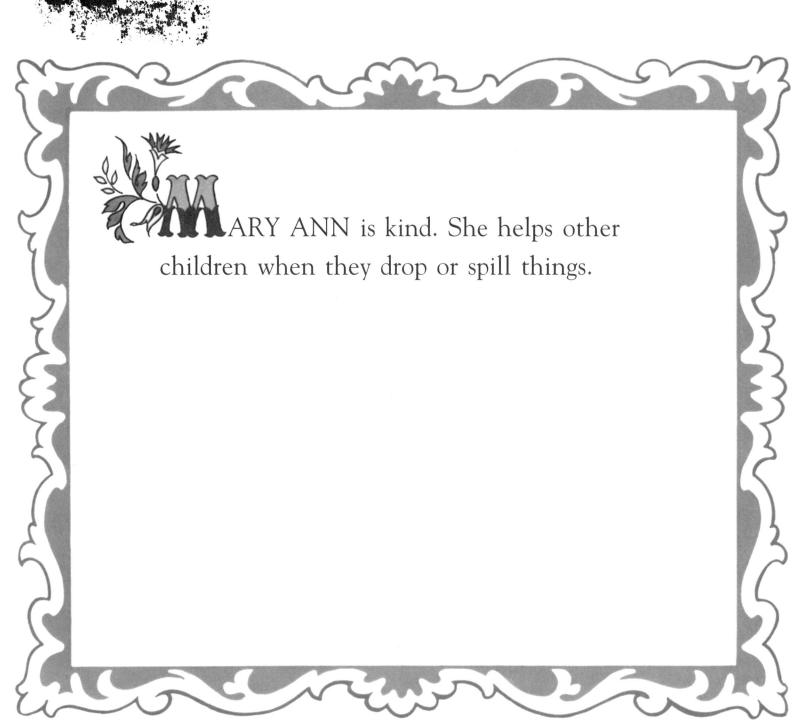

MARY ANN is kind. She helps other children when they drop or spill things.

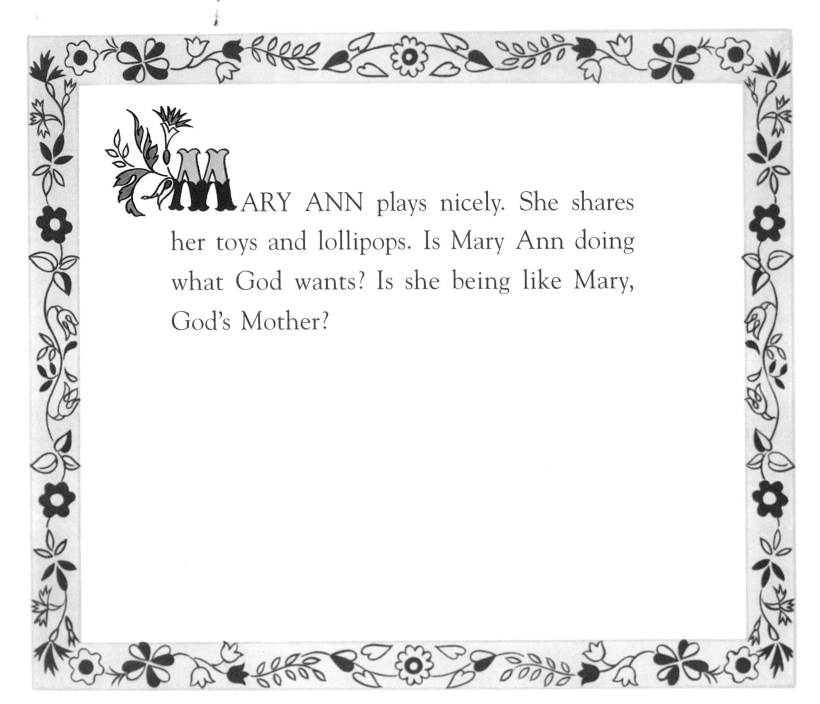

MARY ANN plays nicely. She shares her toys and lollipops. Is Mary Ann doing what God wants? Is she being like Mary, God's Mother?

OW FOLD your hands and close your eyes. God is listening. Whisper: "Dear God, I want to be like Mary, Our Blessed Mother, too. I want to do what You want all day long. Please help me."

FRIENDS IN THE ZOO

A friendly [keeper] went to the zoo every day to feed the animals. He knew what they liked to eat and what was good for them. Sometimes he brought a [banana] for the [monkey], or a [carrot] for the [deer]. He liked to feed the [sea lion] a [fish], and he fed [peanuts] to the [squirrel] and bread crumbs to the [pigeons].

PARROT MONKEY ELEPHANT DEER PEACOCK SEA LION PIGEONS SQUIRREL LION ZEBRA BEAR KANGAROO

He did not feed all the animals, but he talked to each one of them. He talked to the [lion] and to the big, brown [bear]. He visited the [zebra] and the [kangaroo] with the little one in its pouch. The [peacock] showed its beautiful [tail] when the [keeper] came, and the [parrot] said: "Polly wants a cracker." The [elephant] begged for a treat, but there was a sign: Do Not Feed. So the [keeper] only waved, and the [elephant] waved back with its trunk, which meant: Come again!

ROVER, THE MISSING BOOT

Richard was older than his baby sister, Susan, but he still played with a teddy bear, whom he called "Snoozer." He even slept with Snoozer, so that Snoozer need not be afraid of the dark.

But Richard *never* put his things where they belonged—especially his shoes. They got lost almost every day. When he went to bed he used to fling them off his feet just *any-where*.

Daddy did not like to be asked every morning, "Have you seen Richard's shoes?" So, when Richard's birthday came around, he gave him a pair of brown leather boots. They had long laces which could be tied to Richard's feet. Now Richard could not fling them, Daddy thought.

Richard was disappointed with his present. He had wished for a pop-gun. That night in bed he asked Snoozer whether he liked boots better than pop-guns. But Snoozer was tired from the birthday party. He did not feel like talking. Soon, both fell asleep.

They woke up early the next morning. Richard whistled as he got dressed, and Snoozer looked happy, because Daddy had promised to take them into town. Then the terrible thing happened. Richard could not find his new boots! At last he found one, huddled in a corner of the bathroom. But the right boot was missing.

This time Daddy got angry. He put the single boot on top of the toy shelf and told Richard he would not take him into town unless he found the other one.

All morning long Richard and Snoozer hunted for the lost boot. At last Father left without them. It was a miserable day! That night Richard cried himself to sleep. And all the time the little left boot stood on top of the toy shelf, looking sad and lonely.

Richard began to dream. He dreamed he heard a strange noise.

Pat-pat-pat went a big noise. And *cris-cris-cris* rustled a small noise behind it, like little mouse paws on a kitchen floor. What could it be!

Just then the moon peered into the window, and in the silvery light Richard and Snoozer could see what made the noise.

Pat-pat-pat hopped the little left boot on top of the toy shelf. And *cris-cris-cris* rustled the laces behind it. It looked very funny!

Richard was about to giggle, when he heard footsteps.

"It sounds like Daddy," he said, "and Mommy and Susan too!"

Before he could say any more the door burst open—and in walked three pairs of shoes! Father's shoes came first. They walked with big steps as Daddy did when he was angry. Next came Mother's shoes. And Baby Susan's little ones came toddling in behind them.

"What is going on?" asked Daddy's shoes with a gruff and leathery voice. They stopped in front of the toy shelf.

"What is going on?" asked Mother's shoes. They spoke with the little squeak which they had had ever since Mommy bought them.

"What is going on?" echoed the baby shoes with soft and pinkish voices, for they were made of satin.

"What is going on?" asked Father's shoes again. "Who has been calling?"

"I have!" said the lonely little boot. Suddenly he jumped *plunk!* to the floor.

That frightened the little shoes so that they hid in Mother's big ones. They only peered out with their button eyes.

"Shame on you, frightening the Tinies, you—*you loafer!*" gruffed Father's shoes. They were both wearing their laces like a moustache and looked very fierce.

"Tut-tut," creaked Mother's shoes soothingly. "He is only a new one. He doesn't know any better."

The Tinies said nothing. They only blinked their button eyes.

But the Big Ones were still angry.

"A new *one!*" they sneered. "Just look at him—no shine and no pride! Where is your twin, anyway? Don't you know that decent shoes always keep in pairs?"

The poor little boot did not answer. He stood there twisting his laces nervously. Then he began to cry. With his laces he wiped off the dark polish-tears which came oozing out through all the lace-holes. It was a pitiful sight.

Even the Big Ones looked a little less grim now. And the Tinies came out of their hiding places to give the sobbing boot a comforting satiny push.

"Tell us about your twin brother!" said Mother's shoes. Their creaking sounded very gentle. The little boot dried his tears.

"My brother and I lived in a big store," he said. "We slept in a box, filled with soft, clean paper. Oh, how we wished that someone would buy us. We dreamed about how we would be fed polish every day and walk with other shoes on the hard pavement. *Pit-pat-pit-pat* we sang in our sleep. My brother was so eager to see the world. I nicknamed him *Rover* and was very proud of him."

"Tell us what happened to Rover!" begged the Tinies.

The little boot sighed. "When at last we found a customer, we were the proudest boots in the whole world. But our happiness did not last long. Our new master did not care for us. The very first night he flung us into different corners of the bathroom, so that we could not even *see* each other."

"Have you ever heard of such a thing?" snarled the Big Ones.

"Disgusting!" creaked Mother's shoes.

The Tinies whispered what they had been taught: "Decent shoes always keep in pairs." The little boot gave them a hurt look.

"Don't be silly, it wasn't our fault. We tried to get together again. Rover signaled me with his laces and sneaked out through the open door. But before I could catch up with him, somebody closed the door. I never saw him again."

"It is not fair that any shoe should be treated like that!" shouted the Big Ones. In their excitement they were stamping the floor. "It is not fair!" agreed Mother's shoes.

"It is not fair!" echoed the Tinies as they tried to stamp the floor too.

Father's shoes stopped stamping. "We are going on strike," they said. "We are going to demonstrate! Everybody follow us!"

Before the Tinies could ask what the big words meant, they had marched out of the room. All the other shoes followed. *Left-right-left-right* they could be heard marching down the stairs. *Left-right-left-right*—out of the house and into the street.

Richard had seen and heard everything. Suddenly a terrible thought came to his mind.

What if all the shoes in town joined in the strike? What if all the people woke up in the morning and found their shoes gone? Richard jumped out of bed.

"Come on, Snoozer!" he said, "we've got to get them back!"

The night was cold and the sky was full of stars. Everything looked strange and different. Richard stopped.

"Snoozer, did you hear marching shoes?"

Snoozer had heard them too. *Left-right-left-right*—they sounded very heavy. Now they came around the corner. But—oh, dear me—it was Mr. Jones, the policeman! If only he would not see them.

But Mr. Jones had sharp eyes.

"Hello!" he called with surprise. "First I meet a lonely little boot, and now a little boy with a teddy bear. Well, well, well! What is going on in our town?"

When Richard saw the little boot in Mr. Jones's hand he forgot to be afraid.

"Please, Sir, he belongs to me. It's Rover!" Then he told the policeman everything that had happened.

Mr. Jones laughed. "So this is Rover, the runaway boot! You better take him home, because who ever heard of a policeman arresting a boot?"

Then Mr. Jones looked serious again. "To bed with you, before you catch a cold," he grumbled. "I don't want to see any more roving shoes or boys in the middle of the night."

Mr. Jones continued on his round. Richard put the little boot on his foot.

"I wish you could help me to find the others!" he said.

And Rover did. *Pit-pit-pit* he called, walking on the pavement. And *Pat-pat-pat* came an answer, far away at first, but coming closer all the time. *Right-left-right-left*—and at last the whole procession of shoes came hurrying down the street. The little left boot was in front now. Richard quickly put him on his other foot. Now the twins could talk to each other. *Pit-pat-pit-pat* they chatted as they led the other shoes all the way home.

When Richard woke up in the morning he could hardly remember what he had dreamed. But when he saw his new boots standing by his bedside—the right one to the right, and the left one to the left, close together as good twins should be—he knew that everything was fine. Richard and Snoozer were happy.

how would you play

if you had no toys or games or books?

Sometimes when we were tired of our toys we would play "seeing things." One can play it anywhere. One simply looks at whatever there may be: a wooden table top, an ink-spot, the floor, the wallpaper, a tree—anything will do.

When one looks at a thing for a long time very carefully, one begins to see things one never noticed before. If one looks carefully, and then uses a little imagination, the grain in the wood or the ink-spot on the table may look like a landscape; the shadow on the ground may resemble an animal; and maybe the tree seems to have a face with a beard or a crown! The base of the lamp may be like the stairs of a monument. A little dish may look like a swimming pool for dolls.

When we played "seeing things," we would each try to see something. As soon as somebody discovered something interesting, he would say: "I am seeing a bear," or "I am seeing a little man on stilts"—or whatever it was he saw. Now all the others had to try to see the same. Some children found it difficult, even if it was pointed out to them. That is because everybody looks at things differently, and that is a very important part of the fun! Sometimes somebody might say: "That looks like a frog, eating a horse." Then somebody else would shout: "It isn't a frog at all—it looks like a railroad car!" And a third player might say: "The way I see it, it really looks more like a rocking-horse with a broken rocker."

Have you ever tried seeing things? You'll make many discoveries. And when you play it with other people, you may learn to see things through their eyes, too.

THE TWO-WEATHER HOUSE

A frog and a mouse built a little house.
    They used leaves for the floor
    and a hole for the door
    and a mushroom for the roof,
    to make it waterproof.

When the roof was on, there was only room for one,
the house was too small for two!
So what did the builders do?
Do you think they sat down and cried?
Oh no! The frog slept inside on every *sunny* day.
(Because he liked the cool shade of the house.)

But when it *rained*,
the mouse curled up inside like a ball.
(For he didn't like rain at all!)
When it was *sunny*,
    the mouse pattered around the house.
(I mean *outside* the door.)
But the minute it started to *pour*
the mouse slipped inside again,
while the frog sat out in the rain,
    soaking all day long,
      croaking a happy song.
Whatever the weatherman said,
    one of them stayed in bed
while the other enjoyed the fresh air.
Weren't they a clever pair?

THE MERCHANT FROM PARIS

This is a very simple game and can be lots of fun. You can play anywhere—even while doing the dishes. If there are more than two players, you simply take turns being "customers." The last one out becomes merchant.

I'm the merchant from Paris,

I have beautiful things.

Whatever you want—be it sables or rings—

is yours for the asking,

I'll quote you the price.

And also I'll give you this bit of advice:

Some words in this game are forbidden to say:

Yes, No, Black or *White* do not use while you play;

I can say what I please, for the merchant am I—

But *you* must avoid them, nor *laugh, smile* or *cry!*

FOR EXAMPLE

Merchant. "Good morning, lady, what can I do for you?"

Customer. "I would like a pair of shoes."

M. "Certainly, Madam. May I show you a pair? Here—these are big enough for an elephant. Do you like them?"

C. "Thank you, not really. I am looking for a pair for my husband."

M. "Very good. Here are some nice ones. Would you prefer the purple ones or the black ones?"

C. "The second pair you showed me are much prettier."

M. "The black ones?"

C. "Of course!"

M. "Very well. Anything else? A hand-carved necktie or a musical handkerchief?"

C. "Not today, thank you. How much do I owe you?"

M. "That will be $250.31."

C. "That's too much! I'll take another pair."

M. "The purple ones?"

C. "No, the same color, but less expensive."

M. "You said *No!* Now it's your turn to be the merchant!"

 # ORANGE PEOPLE

Orange People are friendly people. Anybody who has a glass, a strong paper napkin, an orange and two raisins (or buttons) in the house can make one of these Orange People.

With a teaspoon or knife make some half-moon incisions for the eyes, the nose and the ears. Cut away some of the peel where the mouth is supposed to be. Lift up the "eyelids," so that you can slide the flattened raisins (or buttons) underneath them. Then carefully lift the ears and nose, to make them stick out.

Cover the glass with the paper napkin and place the orange-head on top of it. By gently tugging at the napkin in different places and directions, you can make the funny little fellow nod or shake his head. At other times he may look shy or sleepy. If you know a nice song, sing it for him, and let him act as if he were singing it himself!

WUPSY GOES TO A MEETING

Soon after the Bishop found he could start a mission in Matongu, the Guardian Angels decided to call a meeting to discuss how they could help. The Angels really did not need to get together, but they liked to gather every now and again to talk things over.

It was a beautiful moonlit night, and after seeing that all the people in Matongu were sound asleep, they met on a nice soft cloud.

Wupsy was a little late because he had to blow a lot of mosquitos away from Sunny before he could get to sleep. They were buzzing around his head and making an awful racket. When he had blown them all away, Wupsy set up a little breeze that would keep the mosquitos out of Sunny's house for the whole night. Then he flew off to the meeting.

The Angels were quite excited about the letter the Bishop had written to Father George, and this is pretty much what they talked about.

"We've all heard the good news," began one of the bigger Angels. "Wupsy has managed it all, and it seems to me that he has done a very good job. In just a few weeks the missioners will be coming to Matongu, and we can rest a little. But between now and then there will be lots to do. Has anyone noticed anything lately?"

286

"Yes, of course," answered one of the other Angels. "The devils are particularly busy trying to make the most of the time that is left to them, because it will be hard for them afterwards. I've met one or two lately, sneaking around in the shadows. Thank goodness I was able to get rid of them before they did any real harm."

"There's that fellow Pong, who is always going after the children," said another Angel. "If he were not such a coward, he would do a lot of harm."

"I've caught another one," said a fourth Angel, "actually collecting fever mosquitoes and spreading them around to make people ill. I had an awful time blowing them all away."

"There is still going to be trouble," said Wupsy, very seriously. "You may be sure the devils will do all they can to spoil things at the beginning. The Guardian Angels will all have to help each other."

"That's important!" agreed another Angel. "We must make sure that things go well at the beginning. Some of the people will want to help the devils all they can. Wupsy won't have much trouble with Sunny, but he'd better look out for strange devils. You never know what might happen."

Then Wupsy told them he had already discovered the devils at a meeting, but before they could make many plans he had chased them all the way to Upper Egypt and had given them headaches that would last three weeks!

The Angels talked about lots of other things, and then they praised God together because the missioners were coming at last.

There was never a happier crowd of Angels! The song they sang went straight to Heaven like smoke from the incense in a church, so the Angels in Heaven looked down to see what was happening in Matongu.

Of all the Angels at the meeting, Wupsy was the happiest, for he was the only one who had a bright soul to take care of. Sunny was the only person in Matongu who had been baptized! Wupsy was hoping and praying that now his hopes and dreams for Sunny might come true. He knew that God had an important job for Sunny!

Continued from inside front cover

No angel ever had to go to school. The angel takes in "at a glance" a vast panorama of knowledge and understanding. Yet he can advance in knowledge.

THE FALLEN ANGELS

Wouldn't you think, now, that such a superior creature would be above temptation?—that he would be too wise to commit sin?

But God gave all His angels free choice. They were free to take Heaven or leave it, and—mysteriously—some of the Angels turned their back on it. Saint Thomas Aquinas thinks that theirs was a sin of pride.

Their punishment was immediate. They were forever banned from the joyous presence of God. Their existence now had lost all point.

Well, to take Lucifer, here was an archangel condemned to contemplate his own stupid sin and failure forever. He would never have another chance. His existence was hopelessly ruined—through his own fault.

At the same time, he was condemned to the everlasting fires of Hell, which were enabled for this occasion, at least, to burn and sear a spiritual substance—unremitting torture through all eternity, freely chosen.

With Lucifer in Hell are those kindred spirits, wicked angels, who joined him in rebellion against God. There they rule a kingdom which is just the reverse of the heavenly home from which they have exiled themselves. Where Heaven is a kingdom of love and order, of peace and truth and justice, Hell is a house of hatred, of disorder and strife, of lying and every injustice. No friendship is possible in Hell, where each spirit is walled within himself in a furious contempt for those around him, brought about by his own misdeeds.

THE DEVIL'S POWER

Through hatred and envy, the Devil and his hordes are constantly seeking to bring about our supernatural death. Our three sources of spiritual trouble are the world, the flesh and the Devil. He can influence our imagination, our nerves, glands and bodily organism—but he cannot move our will. He can stir up our emotions, cause us to feel depressed, and make us bored with our prayers and daily routine.

Why does God permit it? Saint John Chrysostom says that there is little to fear, really, since we have the means of overcoming the Devil, and temptation urges a man on to virtue, keeps him vigilant, humble and united to God in prayer. All in all, it adds to God's glory and our own.

Again, we must never underestimate the Devil's power. Saint Peter says that he goes around "like a roaring lion, seeking whom he may devour," and Saint Paul says, "For our wrestling is not against flesh and blood; but against principalities and powers, against the rulers of the world of this darkness, against the spirits of wickedness in the high places." (*Ephesians* 6:12).

FATHER GINDER

The Story about an Angel was first told by Father Gerard F. Scriven, a White Father, who knew Sunny and his mother and father in Africa. The story is retold as *The Story of Wupsy* for TREASURE BOX.

PEEKING SUE

Today I'll introduce to you
a friend of mine, called Peeking Sue.
Her little face is pink and rosy.
She is a dear—but is she nosy!
Whenever Sue hears people speak
inside a room, she has to peek.
They told her that it isn't nice,
but Susie will not heed advice.
They told her, "You'll get hurt some day!"
But Peeking Sue peeks anyway.
When once again she peeked inside,
the door was being opened wide,
ZOOM! landed Susie on the floor.
They say that now she peeks no more.

TAN

ISBN 0-89555-559-X